THE YOUNG MAN OF CURY

Charles Causley

THE YOUNG MAN OF CURY

and other poems

ILLUSTRATED BY MICHAEL FOREMAN

MACMILLAN CHILDREN'S BOOKS

To
Susan and John Wickett

First published 1991 by
MACMILLAN CHILDREN'S BOOKS
A division of Macmillan Publishers Ltd
London and Basingstoke
Associated companies throughout the world

ISBN 0-333-53812-9

Photoset by Rowland Phototypesetting Ltd
Bury St Edmunds, Suffolk
Printed in Hong Kong

Acknowledgements

"King Ezra" first appeared in *Island of the Children* (Orchard
Books) "Sam Groom" in *Ten Golden Years* (Walker Books) and
"The Obby Oss" in Charles Causley's *Figure of 8* (Macmillan).
"Steam in the Kettle" was originally broadcast in the BBC TV
series *Play School*.

ERRATUM

Contents

A Sort of People

I Saw Charlie Chaplin

I saw Charlie Chaplin
In 1924
Playing golf with a walking-cane
Outside our front door.

His bowler was a size too early,
His trousers were a size too late,
His little moustache said one o'clock,
His boots said twenty-past eight.

He whacked at a potato.
It broke in the bouncing air.
"Never mind, Charlie," I said to him.
"We've got some to spare."

I fetched him out a potato.
He leaned on his S-shaped cane.
"Thanks, kid." He bowed. He shrugged.
I never saw him again.

My father said Charlie Chaplin
Wasn't Charlie at all.
He said it was someone in our town
Going to a Fancy Ball.

He said it couldn't be Charlie.
That it was Carnival Day.
That Charlie never came to our town,
And he lived in the USA.

Not Charlie Chaplin?
You can tell that tale to the cat.
I don't care what my father said.
I know better than that:

For I saw Charlie Chaplin
Outside our front door
Playing golf with a walking-cane.
It was 1924.

King Ezra

King Ezra was a drover
Walked the grey miles to town,
His sceptre was a hazel stick,
A billycock his crown.

His head was whiter than the frost,
His beard white as the floe;
He stood as strong as a stone man
Of Michelangelo.

A sack about his shoulders
In summer and in snow,
And on each foot an army boot
Was splintered at the toe.

Gently he drove the cattle
And softly led the sheep
As he went up to market
Under the Castle Keep.

And if the flock was hasty
Or herd was slow to hand,
He spoke the secret language
All creatures understand.

And never a one would wander
And never a one would stray
As he passed by our window
On Cattle Market Day.

I never heard him call nor cry
Nor saw him strike a blow,
Though in his hand the hazel wand
Was stern as iron crow.

Of all the men to come my way
In days of storm, of calm,
King Ezra wears for me the crown,
King Ezra bears the palm.

I see him as I saw him then
Seasons and worlds ago:
The Good King Ezra whose true name
I never was to know.

The Song of Kruger the Cat

I really hate the coal-man.
I hate his hood and sack.
I'm sure one day he'll carry me off
In a bundle on his back.

When he crunches up to the bunker
And I hear the coal go *crump*
My legs turn into custard
And my heart begins to bump.

I'm not afraid of a bulldog,
A gull or a giant rat,
The milkman or the postman,
Or the plumber, come to that.

But when I hear the coal-man
I shake and quake with fright,
And I'm up and away for the rest of the day
And sometimes half the night.

I'm certain that to his family
He's loving and good and kind,
But when I hear his hobnailed boots
I go right out of my mind.

"Now Kruger, dear," they say, "look here:
Isn't it rather droll?
You love to sleep and snore before
A *fire* that's made of coal."

But I can't help my feelings
However hard I try.
I really hate the coal-man.
Who's that? Good grief! Good-bye!

Pepper and Salt

Pepper and salt his whiskers,
Pepper and salt his hair,
Pepper and salt the three-piece suit
He always likes to wear.

Pepper and salt his muffler,
His hat, and furthermore
Pepper and salt his overcoat
That hangs behind the door.

Pepper and salt his voice is,
Pepper and salt his eye
As he reads out the register
And we pepper and salt reply.

Pepper and salt his singing
When he rises from his chair
And sets to work with a tuning-fork
And a pepper and salty prayer.

He peppers and salts the blackboard
With every kind of sum,
The names of the British Kings and Queens
And the order in which they come.

With a pepper and salty finger
He stabs the maps and charts
And shows us capes and rivers and straits
In home and foreign parts.

Pepper and salt his spectacles,
And it's peppery salty plain
That pepper and salt is his hand of chalk
And pepper and salt his cane.

But silent now the school bell
That Pepper and Salt would sound,
And vanished is the school to which
We came from miles around.

And we who were village children,
Now white of head or hair,
Can never go down the Old School Lane
But Pepper and Salt is there –

Standing in the school-yard
Where weeds and grasses win:
Every day, old Pepper and Salt
Seeing the children in.

There was an Old Woman

There was an old woman of Whittingham Firth
Who hadn't a friend on the face of the earth,
Or so all the people who lived thereabout
Were perfectly certain and hadn't a doubt.

"To get to her cottage," they all would explain,
"You must walk to the end of Deepwatery Lane,
You must cross seven meadows and climb seven stiles
And there isn't a neighbour for miles and miles."

The folk in the village said, "Isn't it sad?
That silly old thing must be really quite mad!
A body must be in a terrible plight
With no-one to talk to from morning till night.

"Though we're none of us gossips, we vow and declare
There's tittle and tattle that all like to share.
It must be like living your life in a doze
With never a notion of how the world goes."

But the little old woman who lived in the cot
Hadn't time to be lonely or time to be not,
For what with one thing and another, it's true,
She'd never a minute with nothing to do.

Each morning the moment that day had begun
She rose from her pillow as sharp as the sun,
And if skies they were shining or skies they were dour
She'd put on the kettle at just the same hour.

When breakfast was done, and the dishes done too,
She'd sweep and she'd polish her little house through.
She baked and she cooked, and as sweet as a dream
She worked her green garden that lay by the stream.

The robin and blackbird they came at her call
And so did the hedgehog lived under the wall,
And every creature came passing that way
She gave them a smile and she spoke them good-day.

And good-night to the moon every evening she said
As, her cat coming after, she went to her bed:
That lonely old woman of Whittingham Firth
Who hadn't a friend on the face of the earth.

Brigid

Brigid, bring the cows
From the water shore
Now the sun is falling
Underneath the moor.

Bring them by the field-oak,
Bring them by the stone
That stands at the cross-way
With Bible pictures on.

In her hand she carries
A wand of green bay
As she brings the swaying herd
Slowly on its way.

The wild duck from their swimming,
The wild duck as they fly
Come at her calling
As she passes by.

Brigid, bring the cows
From the long shore,
Bring the milk and butter
To the hungry poor.

St Brigid of Ireland is said to have founded the first nunnery in that country in about the sixth century. This was at Cill-Dara (the Church of the Oak), also now known as Kildare. Many legends and stories are told of her compassion, one of which is that as a farm-child she was sent by her parents to milk the cows, but gave away all the milk to the poor.

Season and Place

Quarter-jacks

Tom and Tim the quarter-boys
On the Guildhall Tower
Turn and strike the quarter-bell
Twenty times an hour.
Over the swimming river
They stare as straight as light
Except when Tom turns to the left
And Tim turns to the right.
They stand as stiff as iron
Above the moving bay
Waiting for the quarter
And to beat the time away.
Their bonnets are black, are scarlet,
Their suits are yellow, are blue,
Their collars and cuffs are silver
As the buckle on each shoe,
And on the Guildhall Tower
In weather foul or clear
They stand as smart as Sunday
All through the year.
Whether the sun is shining
Or if the moon is high
They stand their ground above the town
Under a Cornish sky.
The day that I first saw them
Is a day long sped,
And never a word I spoke, for there
Was nothing to be said.
The day that I first saw them
Is a day long done
And those who stood beside me
Silent are and gone.
Tom and Tim the quarter-boys
On the Guildhall Tower

Still they strike the quarter-bell
Twenty times an hour:
Tom and Tim the quarter-boys
Standing side by side
Over the changing water,
The turning of the tide.

Out in the Desert

Out in the desert lies the sphinx
It never eats and it never drinx
Its body quite solid without any chinx
And when the sky's all purples and pinx
(As if it was painted with coloured inx)
And the sun it ever so swiftly sinx
Behind the hills in a couple of twinx
You may hear (if you're lucky) a bell that clinx
And also tolls and also tinx
And they say at the very same sound the sphinx
It sometimes smiles and it sometimes winx:

But nobody knows just what it thinx.

Frost on the Flower

Frost on the flower,
Leaf and frond,
Snow on the field-path,
Ice on the pond.

Out of the east
A white wind comes.
Hail on the rooftop
Kettledrums.

Snow-fog wanders
Hollow and hill.
Along the valley
The stream is still.

Thunder and lightning.
Down slaps the rain.
No doubt about it.
Summer again.

Tam Snow

(to Kaye Webb)

Who in the bleak wood
Barefoot, ice-fingered,
Runs to and fro?
> *Tam Snow.*

Who, soft as a ghost,
Falls on our house to strike
Blow after blow?
> *Tam Snow.*

Who with a touch of the hand
Stills the world's sound
In its flow?
> *Tam Snow.*

Who holds to our side,
Though as friend or as foe
We never may know?
> *Tam Snow.*

Who hides in the hedge
After thaw, waits for more
Of his kind to show?
> *Tam Snow.*

Who is the guest
First we welcome, then
Long to see go?
> *Tam Snow.*

Bird and Beast

Turnstone

Turnstone, tangle picker,
Sifting the ocean,
Wading the water,
Tipping the stone,
Always you stand
At the brink of the billows,
Neither in deep
Nor on the high strand.

"What is your story?"
I asked of the turnstone
Careful, aware-ful
Between sea and shore;
But all that I heard
Was a chuckle, a twitter,
Nor deep, nor high,
Nothing less, nothing more.

Aireymouse

Aireymouse, wary mouse,
Steering and veering
At sunrise and sunfall
By tower and tree,
Is it because
You appear to be *peering*
The old wives all said
That you never could see?

Flying mouse, skying mouse,
Neatly and featly,
Skilfully, sweetly
You dive and you dare,
But who was the noddy
Who told everybody
That if you came near
You would lodge in my hair?

Swooping mouse, looping mouse,
Curving and swerving,
Here-ing and there-ing
Now low, now high,
Soft in your silky coat
Through the wild air you float:
Aireymouse, wary mouse
Passing me by
Tell me, O tell me,
Who taught you to fly?

"Aireymouse" is the country name for a bat; in this case, the
pipistrelle.

Python on Piccolo

Python on piccolo,
Dingo on drums,
Gannet on gee-tar*
Sits and strums.

Croc on cornet
Goes to town,
Sloth on sitar
Upside-down.

Toad on tuba
Sweet and strong,
Crane on clarinet,
Goat on gong.
  And the sun jumped up in the morning.

Toucan travelling
On trombone,
Zebra zapping
On xylophone.

Beaver on bugle
Late and soon,
Boa constrictor
On bassoon.

Tiger on trumpet
Blows a storm,
Flying fox
On flügelhorn.
And the sun jumped up in the morning.

Frog on fiddle,
Hippo on harp,
Owl on oboe
Flat and sharp.

Viper on vibes
Soft and low,
Pelican
On pi-a-no.

Dromedary
On double-bass,
Cheetah on 'cello
Giving chase.
And the sun jumped up in the morning.

* *guitar*

Tell Me the Time

"Tell me the time," the wok-wok sang
Flying the China Sea.
"Ten to eleven? Don't say that!
I thought it was half-past three."

"Tell me the day," the tyg-tyg called
From the Great Australian Bight.
"Monday morning? Gracious me!
It feels like Saturday night."

"Tell me the date," the tass-tass cried
As it circled above Rangoon.
"First of March? According to me
It's the twenty-fourth of June."

"Tell me the year," the cran-cran sighed
Swimming by Timbuktu.
"1999? I'm sure
It's 1802."

And with a small frown each went the same
                                    way
The seconds and years had gone.
There really was no more to say,
And the great globe rolled on.

Dartford Warbler

Stay-at-home
  Never-roam
    Dartford warbler
Hiding in furze
  On the yellow plain,
    Skulking in scrub,
Secret in heather
  As seasons turn
    And turn again;

Spending your day
  On the highest spray
    Or sprig or twig
Where you first
  Saw day;
    Wearing the English
Storm and summer,
  Never, ever
    To fly away.

Restless, hole-in-
    The-corner creeper,
        I watch in spring
When you bob
    Like a ball
        High on the bush-top
Singing, scattering
    Rattling music
        Over all.

Slate-wing, starveling
    Beyond my window,
        Cheery, unweary
In sun, in snow,
    Packed my bag
        I hear you crying,
"You too! You too!
    Tell me, spell me
        Why do you go?"

I Don't Want to Grumble

"I don't want to grumble," said Sally the Mouse.
"I don't want to grumble at all,
And I don't want to grouse, but they've
                    brought home a HOUSE
And it hangs on the living-room wall.

"It's painted and polished as clean as a pin,
But here's something that gave me a shock:
From somewhere within there's a sound that's akin
To a curious tick and a tock.

"And the worst of the matter (of this there's
                    no doubt)
Is each day and each night, through and through,
There's a terrible shout from a bird that flies out
And calls everybody cuckoo!"

"Such conduct," said Sally, "is simply absurd
As I frequently try to explain,
But that ill-mannered bird just ignores every word
And flies forwards *and backwards* again.

"My children can't sleep and their heads they are sore
And our dear little homestead they shun.
I'm not at all sure I can stand any more.
Will you please tell me what's to be done?"

Wise and Foolish

Old Billy Ricky

Old Billy Ricky
Lives down a well
Snug as a silver
Snail in a shell,
Sits all day
On a mossy shelf
Keeping himself
(He says) to himself,
Whistles and watches
The circle of sky
As weathers and seasons
Pass him by.

Nothing to eat
But plenty to drink,
How can he ever
Sleep a wink,
Back pressed tight
To a ferny wall
Nothing to catch him
If he should fall,
And what for mercy's
Sake can he see
In a newt and a frog
For company?

But there he sits
In his round stone room
The green moss glimmering
In the gloom,
And if you should ask
On the village square
How long Billy's
Been down there
There's nobody knows
Wherefore or why
And if you ask *him*
You won't get a reply:
He simply won't answer,
He never will tell
Won't old Billy Ricky.

Well! Well! Well!

Don't Wake Up Lord Hazey

Don't wake up Lord Hazey,
Let him take his rest.
Let him snore – I'm certain sure
It's really for the best.

Don't wake up Lord Hazey,
Don't bother him at all.
I don't think he'd appreciate
An early-morning call.

Don't wake up Lord Hazey,
Let him dream and doze.
Don't take up a tea and toast
And don't lay out his clothes.

Don't wake up Lord Hazey,
I wouldn't think it wise
However shines the midday sun,
However blue the skies.

Don't wake up Lord Hazey,
Don't give him a shake.
There's just no knowing what he'll do
When he's wide awake.

Don't wake up Lord Hazey,
Don't give his door a knock
Whoever's on the telephone
Or what it is o'clock.

Don't wake up Lord Hazey,
And don't get in a fizz;
Better to leave Lord Hazey
Exactly where he is.

Mrs Malarkey

Mrs Malarkey
(Miss Rooke, that was)
Climbed to the top of a tree
And while she was there
The birds of the air
Kept her company.

Her friends and her family
Fretted and fumed
And did nothing but scold and sneer
But Mrs Malarkey
She smiled and said,
"I'm perfectly happy up here.

"In this beautiful nest
Of sticks and straw
I'm warmer by far than you,
And there's neither rent
Nor rates to pay
And a quite indescribable view.

"A shield from the snow
And the sun and rain
Are the leaves that grow me round.
I feel safer by far
On this green, green spar
Than ever I did on the ground."

Mrs Malarkey
She covered herself
With feathers of purple and blue.
She flapped a wing
And began to sing
And she whistled and warbled too.

And the birds of the air
Brought seed and grain
And acorns and berries sweet,
And (I must confirm)
The occasional worm
As an extra special treat.

"Mrs Malarkey!
Come you down!"
The people all cried on the street.
But, *Chirrupy, chirrup*
She softly sang,
And, *Tweet, tweet,
Tweet, tweet, tweet.*
Chirrupy, chirrup
(As smooth as syrup)
And, *Tweet, tweet,
Tweet, tweet, tweet.*

Send for Solomon Fingergreen

Send for Solomon Fingergreen
As fast as you can go
For nothing in the garden
Is looking like to grow.
When I got up at dawning
The sun was rising bright
But everything in the garden
It looked a sorry sight.
When I looked out at noonday
The morning sun had shone
But everything in the garden
Was looking wisht* and wan.

Send for Solomon Fingergreen,
Ring his front door bell,
Tell him that the garden
Is looking far from well.
Ask him to bring his barrow,
His fork and spade and hoe,
And what's to nip and what's to snip
He's very sure to know.
Ask him to bring his dibble,
His mattock and his bill,
For it seems to me the garden
Is looking rather ill.

Send for Solomon Fingergreen,
Fetch him at the run,
For only Solomon Fingergreen
Will know what's to be done,
For Solomon has the country tongue,
And silent he will say,
And all green things will listen
And all green things obey,
Though where he learned the speaking
And how he earned the spell
Is something Solomon Fingergreen
Will never ever tell.

You may think to give him silver
But this he won't allow.
He says it's a gift of the gods, you see,
He got he don't know how.
But if the green of the garden
Is looking far from spry,
"Send for Solomon Fingergreen,"
Is what the neighbours cry.
"Send for Solomon Fingergreen
Who year by turning year
Speaks the deep green speeches
That everything green will hear."

* *wisht* = unwell or sad

Annabel-Emily

Annabel-Emily Huntington-Horne
Who lives at Threepenny Cam
From the very first moment that she was born
Would eat nothing whatever but jam.

They offered her milk, they offered her bread,
They offered her biscuits and beans
But Annabel-Emily shook her head
And made the most horrible scenes.

They offered her chicken, and also a choice
Of sausage or cheese or Spam
But Annabel screamed at the top of her voice,
"Can't you see what I'm wanting is JAM?"

Her parents they wept like the watery bay
And they uttered and spluttered such cries
As, "She's perfectly certain to waste away
In front of our very own eyes!"

But Annabel-Emily Huntington-Horne,
Her hair the colour of snow,
Still lives in the cottage where she was born
A hundred years ago.

Her tooth is as sugary sweet today
As ever it was before
And as for her hundred years, they say
She's good for a hundred more.

She's pots of apricot, strawberry, peach
In twos and threes and fours
On yards and yards of shelves that reach
From the ceilings to the floors.

She's jars of currants red and black
On every chest and chair
And plum and gooseberry in a stack
On every step of the stair.

Raspberry, cranberry, blackberry, or
Apple, damson, quince –
There never was better jam before
Nor will ever be better since.

For Annabel of Threepenny Cam,
Whose ways are quite well known,
Has never been one for boughten jam
And always makes her own.

But if, when you are passing by,
She invites you for tea and a treat
Be careful just how you reply
If your taste and tooth aren't sweet:

Or it's certain (all the neighbours warn)
You'll be in a terrible jam
With Annabel-Emily Huntington-Horne
Who lives at Threepenny Cam.

"Spam" is the proprietary name for a particular brand of tinned, spiced ham loaf which first became well known in Britain during the Second World War.
"Boughten" is a dialect word meaning something bought in a shop as opposed to being home-made.

Rory O'Donnell

My friend Mr Rory O'Donnell
Who lives in a house next the sea
Each morning at ten
Retires to his den
And sits silent from breakfast to tea.
And neither a word does he utter
Nor ever a note does he sigh,
But fixes his gaze
In a kind of a daze
On the ocean or maybe the sky.

And sometimes he taps with his fingers
Or waves them about in the air,
But most of the day
He's contented to stay
Quite perfectly still in his chair.
And now and again as he listens
A look in his eye makes it clear
That he's suddenly found
A strain or a sound
That nobody else seems to hear.

Then he calls out for pencil and paper
And rulers and pens by the score
And he struggles and strives
Drawing lines (all in fives)
And sprinkles them over galore
With sketches of hooks and of hangers
And things like an egg in a shell,
And dashes and dots
And little black blots
And words in *Italian* as well.

There's nobody here is quite certain
What Rory O'Donnell is at,
And the neighbours all say
He sends them away
When they knock on his door for a chat.
Perhaps we should send for a Doctor
Or a Priest or a Vicar should call,
Or maybe a few
Men in Very Dark Blue?
We can't think what he's up to at all.

Sam Groom

What are you writing down there, Sam Groom,
All alone in a deep, damp room,
Nose on the paper, tongue held tight,
What are you writing by candle-light?
  Words, says Sam.
  That's what I am.

Why do you write down there, Sam Groom,
While the bright bees buzz and the roses bloom?
Scribble and scrape goes your pen all day
As the sun and summer waste away.

Are you writing to your mammy or your daddy, Sam Groom,
Squinting your eye in the candle-fume,
To your brother or your sister or your own true-dove
Or a friend or a foe that we know not of?

Is it a sermon or a bill of sale,
A shilling-shocker or a nursery-tale?
Is it blank, blank verse or a tally of rhymes
Or a letter to the Editor of *The Times*?

Are you putting the wrongs to rights, Sam Groom,
As you sit in a kitchen as chill as the tomb?
Is it songs for the owl or songs for the lark
Or a tune to whistle against the dark?

They say that you'll stay where you are, Sam Groom,
From half past nothing to the day of doom.
What are you writing down there, Sam Groom,
All alone in a deep, damp room?
  Words, says Sam.
  That's what I am.

At Sea

What Sailors Say

Whistle in calm, the wind shall wail.
Whistle in breeze shall bring a gale.

Priest nor parson ship-board tread.
These are buriers of the dead.

Sure is he from wind and weather
If he wear the wild wren's feather.

Flowers fresh upon the blue,
Ship is lost and all her crew.

Carry a maid against the swell
She shall keep and guard you well.

The carving of a woman as a figurehead over the cutwater of a ship was believed to be a charm against severe storms.

How the Sea

"How the sea does shout,"
Says Danny Grout.
"Sounds very vexed.
What does it say?"
　Feed me a wreck,
　Said Sam-on-the-Shore.

"How the sea cries,"
Says Jimmy Wise.
"Early and late.
What does it say?"
　Send me some freight,
　Said Sam-on-the-Shore.

"How the sea moans,"
Said Johnnie Stones
Growing pale, then paler.
"What does it say?"
　Send me a sailor,
　Said Sam-on-the-Shore.

"Shall we sail today?"
Says Dan, says Jim,
Also John.
　Don't fancy a cold swim.
　Homeward we go, boys.
　Put kettle on,
　Said Sam-on-the-Shore.

Three Green Sailors

Three green sailors
Went to sea
In a sailing ship
Called *The Flying Flea*.
Their caps were round,
Their shirts were square,
Their trousers were rolled
And their feet were bare.
One wore a pigtail,
One wore a patch,
One wore ear-rings
That never did match.
One chewed baccy,
One chewed cake,
One chewed a pennyworth
Of two-eyed steak.
One danced to,
One danced fro
And the other sang the shanty
"Haul Away Joe."

They cried "Belay!"
They called "Avast!"
They hoisted the sail
To the top of the mast.
They cast off aft,
They cast off fore
And away they sailed
From the steady shore.
"There's never a doubt,"
Said the sailors three,
"That *this* is the life
For the likes of we!"

But soon it was clear
As clear could be
Three green sailors
Were all at sea:
For nothing they knew
Of star or sun
And nothing of nav-i-
Ga-ti-on,
And they'd no idea
(For they'd never been taught)
Which was starboard
And which was port.
They never did compass
Nor chart possess
Nor a lamp nor a rocket
For an SOS.
But three green sailors
Thought it a ball
And weren't in the least
Bit troubled at all.

The sea rose up,
The light grew thin
And the tide it turned them
Out and in.
The winds blew high
As about they spun
And the thunder sounded
Like a gun.
The Flying Flea
Through the waves it flew
And sometimes *under*
The water too.
In ocean salt,
In ocean cold,
The Flying Flea
It rocked and rolled.

It shook from stem
To stern until
Three green sailors
Were greener still.
"Dear us!" they cried
And "Help!" they roared
As the wind it whined
And the water poured.
"It's a shock," they said,
"To our systems three
How quickly the weather
May change at sea.
Not a minute ago
The sky looked great
And now we're in the middle
Of a gale (force 8).
And another fact
We just can't skip:
We don't know a THING
About seamanship."
So they wept, they cried
And they went all numb
And they felt their very
Last hour had come.

But old King Neptune
Down below
Heard them sobbing
Like billy-o.
He smiled a smile,
He winked an eye
And he said, "I'll give them
One more try,
For sure as a pound
Is a hundred pence
Another time

They'll show more sense
And I've led those lubbers
Such a dance
I think they deserve
Another chance.
But before again
They take to the sea
They really must learn
A thing or three,
For those who sail
The mighty blue
Should be skilled as a seaman
Through and through.
They must learn the trade
From a to zee
Or they'll all end up
Down here with me.''

And now with a blow
Of his salt-sea hand
He washed the good ship
Back to land
And three green sailors
Came ashore
Wiser by far
Than they were before.
"O never," they said,
"Will we sail the brine
In weather that's foul
Or weather that's fine
Till we learn as well
As well can be
The ways of a sailor,
A ship and the sea."
And with knees of jelly
And a wavery tread
Each went home
To his own sweet bed.
And Neptune laughed
On the ocean floor
And he stirred the waters
Just once more.
He stirred the waters,
He sang a salt rhyme
And he stirred the waters
One more time,
For he never will tire,
He never will sleep:
Neptune, Neptune,
King of the Deep.

"Two-eyed steak" is sailors' slang for a bloater or a kipper.

Dreamt Last Night

Dreamt last night of young Jack Swallow
With his fiddle and his bow
Sailed with us in *Kingston Sapphire*
Oceans high and low.

Seas lurched up and seas lurched down,
Sky was strong with wind and rain,
Jack he shrugged and Jack he whistled
"Happy Days Are Here Again".

When the wave was in the messdeck,
When no spuds were in the bin,
When we worked an eight-hour trick
And the bread had weevils in,

When the guns had smoked, and midnight
Burned as brightly as the noon,
Jack it was played "Philadelphia",
"Haul the Bowline", "Bold Dragoon".

Never a word of you, Jack Swallow,
Since our fortune was as one
In cold seas quiet as glass,
Seas the colour of the sun.

Where do you walk today, Jack Swallow?
Is it beneath a stranger star?
Do you lie under the blue, the green,
And is it near or far?

Still I hear your voice, Jack Swallow,
Through the darkness of the day;
Still I hear the songs you sang
And your fiddle play.

A trick is the time a sailor spends on watch or duty. An eight-hour trick is also known as "watch on watch", or "watch on, stop on": that is, on continuous duty for eight hours before a "relief" comes on watch to take your place.

Magic and Spell

How to Protect Baby
from a Witch

Bring a bap
Of salted bread
To the pillow
At his head.
Hang a wreath
Of garlic strong
By the cradle
He lies on.
(Twelve flowers
On each stem
For Christ's good men
Of Bethlehem.)
Dress the baby's
Rocking-bed
With the rowan
Green and red.
(Wicked witch
Was never seen
By the rowan's
Red and green.)
Bring the crystal
Water in,
Let the holy
Words begin,
And the priest
Or parson now
Write a cross
Upon his brow.

Houseleek

Houseleek, houseleek
On the roof-tree
Send away thunder
To the far sea;
Send away lightning,
Send away storm,
Keep all who live here
Free from harm.

Who plants the sengreen,
Jupiter's Beard,
May of witch and wizard
Never have fear.
"Houselick, houselick,"
My grannie would say,
"Lean on my roof-top
Night and day.

"This way, that way
Lean to me,
Welcome-home-husband-
However-drunk-you-be.
Lean in moonlight,
Lean in sun.
Is one drunken husband
Better than none?"

One of the country names for the houseleek or sengreen (a plant once thought to have special magical properties) is "Welcome-home-husband-however-drunk-you-be".

Changeling

No word I ever said,
Nor tear I ever shed;

My skin as fine as silk,
My breath as mild as milk.

Call me of elvish state
My glance shall prick you straight.

Left in my cot a space
Unwashed of hand and face

When once again we meet
I shall be scrubbed and sweet,

My torn and tangled hair
Be brushed and combed and fair.

Though sorrowful my eye
When mortals pass me by,

Watched as I lie alone
My sadness is quite gone,

And I shall laugh and spree
With those you may not see.

Nor beat me with a brier,
Nor burn me with the fire,

Nor leave me on the hill
In weather warm or chill,

For every hope is vain
Your own may come again,

But treat me fit and kind
That others be of mind

Your own dear child and true
Be kindly treated too.

Here, the changeling is an elf-child substituted by fairies for a mortal baby. In earlier times, an infant thought to be a changeling was often very badly treated, or left out in the open, in the hope that the fairy people would exchange it again for the baby originally stolen.

Simples and Samples

"Simples and samples," said the White Witch.
"See what I bear in my pack.
Cures for a quinsy and cures for an itch
And one for a crick in the back.

"One for a toothache and one for a rash,
One for a burn or a scald.
One for a colic and one for a gash,
One for a head that is bald.

"One for a pimple and one for a sore,
One for a bruise or a blow.
One for sciatica, one for a snore,
One for a gathering toe.

"One for a nettle sting, one for a bee,
One for the scratch of a briar.
One for a stomach when sailing the sea,
One for St Anthony's fire."

"White Witch," I said as she stood in the sun,
"Have you a balm or a brew
For a true loving heart that lately was one
And now is quite broken in two?"

The white old Witch shook me her white old head
As down by my side she sat.
"Cures for a thousand, my dear," she said.
"Never a cure for that."

*A simple is a medicine made from a single herb or plant. St Anthony's
fire, also known as "the rose" or "the sacred fire", was a name given
in earlier times to erysipelas, a fever accompanied by an acute
inflammation of the skin. It was a popular belief that cures were
possible through the intercession, by prayer, of St Anthony of Padua.*

Seven Tales of Alder

1

On land, in water
I hold with sound shoot,
Stout-as-stone root,
The wasting hedge,
Bruised river banks.
Farmer, remember.
Give thanks.

2

Soft stream,
Unsleeping river,
Refound my flesh.
Men, women, ever
Use me for soles,
Use me for shoes.
No mud nor rain
Shall enter in,
Nor frost, nor hoar
Seven winters strong,
Seven summers long,
And seven more.

3

Cut my body,
Break a branch
My bright blood
You shall not stanch.
Axe me down,
I rise from ground,
Follow you over
Field and town
Ceasing only
When you leap
Over waters
Swift and deep.

4

Brush with broom
Of alder stem
From Chapman's Well
To Bethlehem
And bring me home
At Come-to-Good
In clogs of yellow
Alder wood.

5

Gather a leaf
(Round as fan)
Dew of morning
Still upon.
Every flea
In hall and home
Shall gather there
And soon be gone.

6

Hear the green song
That I sing.
I am Alder,
I am King,
Green of body,
Green of hair.
Follow me, children,
Woodman, wife,
Follow to the end
Of life;
Follow to the woods
From where
In frost or snow-shine,
Fine or rain,
Never you
Come home again.

7

Woodman, good man,
Make me a rocker
For my cradle
Said Mother Cardle.
See, it's broken and done
And my strength is gone.
Make me a rocker
For my cradle
From the alder you're chopping
For kindle.

Ask *me* first,
Said Alder.
First ask if I'm able
To spare for him
Root or limb,
Branch or bough.
Ask now,
Mother Cardle:
Or baby's bones
Won't grow
A single day
And before he's an hour
Older
His breath will fly
Far away
To a dark land
And colder.
Ask *me* first
If I'm able,
Mother Cardle,
Said Alder.

Questions

Steam in the Kettle

Steam in the kettle,
Steam in the pan,
Tell me, tell me
If you can,
As through the white air
You boil and blow –
Where do you come from
And where do you go?

Steam from a tower,
Steam from a train,
You smudge the sky
And are gone again.
Up in the air
You straggle and fly,
But when I call
You never reply.

Steam in the iron
And in the machine,
Keep my clothes
Both neat and clean;
But when your work
Is over and done
As frail as a ghost
You're faded and gone.

Steam from the pipe
And smoke from the stack,
Send me a signal
Of white or black.
You float like a feather
Over the green,
And then it's as if
You never had been.

Mist in the meadow
And fume in the street
– One so bitter
And one so sweet –
What will you write
On the page of day
Before you silently
Hurry away?

Mist and fume
And smoke and steam
– Wilder than water
From sea or stream –
Wandering low
And wandering high
On city stone
Or in country sky:

I see your breath
On the window-pane,
Or crossing the clouds
Like an aeroplane,
Sometimes near
And sometimes far –
Tell me, tell me
Who you are!

Fume and mist
And steam and smoke –
You never heard
A word I spoke;
But till the seven seas
Stop their flow
And the wheeling world
Is turned to snow,
I'll ask you what
I want to know:
Where do you come from
And where do you go?

Miss Pennyluney

Miss Pennyluney went away
Softly down Quarrywell Lane
In the yellow light of an autumn day
And won't be home again.
The gate is locked, the doors are barred
Both at the front and back,
And there's never a single feather of smoke
Comes out at the chimney stack.
No more I'll hear her feed her hens
In frost or rain or shine,
Or call home Tom her tabby cat
Each evening sharp at nine.
No more she'll hand me through the hedge
An apple red as the sun,
Or every Wednesday (when she bakes)
A home-made saffron bun.
Miss Pennyluney went quite alone
As far as I can tell
The day I heard in Quarrywell Lane
The sound of the minute-bell.

But still I watch the window
That's underneath the thatch
Where Miss Pennyluney looked down at me
And over her garden patch,
And where the hen-roost used to be,
And Tom the tab, and the apple tree.

Trim-and-Tall

Trim-and-Tall
Sat on the mountain,
Dabbled his feet
Where the waves ran in,
Tilted his bonnet,
Stretched his fine fingers
The compass round
For what he might win.

Trim-and-Tall
Speered down the valley,
The twisting river,
The hill, the plain;
Saw people striving,
Loving, living
In every season
Of shine, of rain.

Trim-and-Tall
Watched them raise up
Those who faltered, who fell
In the world's weather;
Saw them cheer
Those who wept,
Journeying always onward
Together, together.

Trim-and-Tall
On the mountain sat,
All he could wish
At his hand in fee.
I saw him there
Lonely and long,
And Trim-and-Tall sighed
Endlessly.

Dream Poem

I have not seen this house before
Yet room for room I know it well:
A thudding clock upon the stair,
A mirror slanted on the wall.

A round-pane giving on the park.
Above the hearth a painted scene
Of winter huntsmen and the pack.
A table set with fruit and wine.

Here is a childhood book, long lost.
I turn its wasted pages through:
Every word I read shut fast
In a far tongue I do not know.

Out of a thinness in the air
I hear the turning of a key
And once again I turn to see
The one who will be standing there.

Dear Me

Dear me, but haven't you heard?
Barnaby Robbins turned into a bird.
His back is brown, his nose is a beak
And there's much more colour come into his cheek.

He's part of him white, and instead of a vest
He's a lot of red feathers all over his chest.
He hasn't a tooth in the whole of his head
And as for toes, he's claws instead.

He bobs his noddle and flirts his tail
As he hops and stops on the orchard rail,
And here's a thing that made me squirm:
I saw him eating a garden worm.

I asked young Barnaby what was wrong
But all he did was sing me a song.
"Barney," I said, "don't take it amiss –
But you simply can't go on behaving like this."

"Barney," I said, "will you listen to me?"
But he flew to the top of the sycamore tree.
"Barney," I said, "you'll be sorry one day."
But he whistled a tune and he flew away.

What Happened

What happened to Jonathan Still,
Cider-sour, all smothered in flour,
Used to work Ridgegrove Mill?
      Off on a long stay
      With gran and grand, they say,
      Under the hill.

Never seem to see Tom Black –
Marched with the men, nineteen-I-don't-know-when –
With rifle and pack.
      Showed his soldier face
      In some foreign space.
      Never came back.

Where's Silly Dick Sloppy, so small, so slim,
Used to mooch by with rod, basket and fly
To doze on the river brim?
      Trying the water
      This year and a quarter,
      Taking a deep swim.

Do you know where is Tamasine Long,
Her with the green stare, the guinea-gold hair?
Went wandering with Singing Ben Strong?
    Never returned –
    Maybe she learned
    A different song.

What happened to Fidgety Goodge, Tinker John,
Little Tim Spy, him with the bad eye,
Beulah and Billy Fireworks, kept *The Swan*?
    Couldn't keep track of 'em,
    Never one of the pack of 'em.
    All gone, gone.

Newlyn Buildings

When we lived in Newlyn Buildings
Half a hundred years ago
Scents and sounds from every quarter
(Sometimes fast and sometimes slow)
Floated through the bricks and mortar.
Though who had the top apartment
No-one ever seemed to know.

On our left, the Widow Whiting
By a curtain fresh as snow
Sat with cotton and with needle
Working at a little treadle
Hard as ever she could go.
Though who had the top apartment
No-one ever seemed to know.

To our right was Catgut Johnson
With a fiddle and a bow,
Sometimes wrong and sometimes right time,
Morning, noon and often night-time
Playing to his tame white crow.
Though who had the top apartment
No-one ever seemed to know.

Underneath lived Annie Fluther,
Family washing all a-blow,
Image of the perfect mother,
Children neat from head to toe
(Six of one and six the other).
Though who had the top apartment
No-one ever seemed to know.

But I heard, in Newlyn Buildings,
Times and seasons long ago,
Overhead each day from dawning,
Through the night from dark to morning,
Footsteps pacing to and fro,
Footsteps old and footsteps new,
To and fro and fro and to.
Though who had the top apartment
No-one ever seemed to know.

Song and Story

The Young Man of Cury

I am the Young Man of Cury,
I lie on the lip of the sand,
I comb the blown sea with five fingers
To call my true-love to the land.

She gave me a comb made of coral,
She told me to comb the green tide
And she would rise out of the ocean
To lie on the strand by my side.

Her hair flowed about her like water,
Her gaze it was blue, it was bold,
And half of her body was silver
And half of her body was gold.

One day as I lay by the flood-tide
And drew the bright comb to and fro
The sea snatched it out of my fingers
And buried it in the dark flow.

She promised me that she would teach me
All the hours of waking, of sleep,
The mysteries of her salt country,
The runes and the tunes of the deep;

How spells may be broken, how sickness
Be cured with a word I might tell,
The thief be discovered, the future
Be plain as these pebbles, this shell.

My son and his son and his also,
She said, would be heir to such charm
And their lives and their loves hold in safety
For ever from evil and harm.

But never a song does she sing me,
Nor ever a word does she say
Since I carried her safe where the tide-mark
Is scored on the sands of the bay.

I am the Young Man of Cury,
I lie on the lip of the sand,
I comb the blown sea with five fingers
To call my true-love to the land.

*Cury is a village near Lizard Point in Cornwall. Cornish legends tell
of how a fisherman from Cury rescued a stranded mermaid and
returned her to the sea. Robert Hunt has a version called ''The Old
Man of Cury'' in his* Popular Romances of the West of England
(1881), set in Kynance Cove, also in the Lizard Peninsula.

Riverside

When you were born at Riverside,
My mother said to me,
It rained for nights, it rained for days
And then some more, said she.

And all at once came riding
The water with a roar
Along the river valley
Down from Bodmin Moor.

The water came in at the window,
It came in at the door,
It swallowed up the cellar,
It came up through the floor.

It filled up every kettle,
It filled up every crock,
It swam around the fireplace,
It filled the long-case clock.

It climbed the kitchen dresser,
It climbed the kitchen chairs,
It climbed up on the table,
It climbed the kitchen stairs.

And as we wailed and wondered
If we should sink or float,
My father came to Riverside
In a sailing-boat.

He took me and my mother
To move upon the swell,
My brother Shem, my brother Ham,
Their families as well.

He took him food and fodder
To sail upon the blue,
He took aboard all creatures
By two and two and two.

And after days and after nights
Watching the waters pour,
We landed on a mountain-top
Somewhere by Wise Man's Tor.

All this, my mother told me,
Was when I was in my pram,
And next door lived my brother Shem,
And next to him lived Ham.

This tale my mother told me
The truth that I might say
Of when I lived at Riverside
Yesterday.

The Obby Oss

Early one morning,
   Second of May,
Up jumped the Obby Oss,
   Said, "I'm away!"

With his tall dunce-head
   And his canvas gown
He tiptoed the streets
   Of Padstow town.

The wild, wild ponies
   Of Bodmin Moor
Said, "Go back, Obby,
   To Padstow shore!

"With your snappers of oak
   And your tail of horse
You can't come running
   On this race-course."

He went to Helston,
   He jigged, he danced,
And in and out
   Of the houses pranced.

"You can't stop here,"
   They said, said they,
"If you won't dance the furry
   In the Helston way."

He went to Brown Willy
   On the Eve of St John.
They said, "Who's that
   With the black kilt on?

''You'll soon run, Obby,
    To your drinking-trough
When the midsummer fire
    Burns your top-knot off!''

He went to St Ives
    Where on the height
Danced ten pretty maids
    All dressed in white.

And round they ran
    To the fiddler's moan
In the waking light
    By John Knill's stone.

He went to St Columb
   For the hurling game.
"You must go back, Obby,
   From where you came!

"For high in the air
   Flies the silver ball,
And Obby can't catch
   Or kick at all."

The County Council
   Gave a county stare,
Said, "Who's that dancing
   With his legs all bare?

"Go back, Obby,
   To Padstow Bar
As quick as the light
   Of a shooting star."

The people of Padstow
   Night and day
Watched for Obby
   Like the first of May.

Without old Obby
   And his dancing drum
They feared that the summer
   Never would come.

When April ended
   At the bell's first beat,
Obby came dancing
   Down the street.

"Welcome, Obby!"
  He heard them cheer,
"For we love you the best
  Of the Padstow year."

"Never again
  Will I run or roam,"
Said Obby, "from Padstow
  My own true home.

"See the sun is rising,
  It dries up the dew,
That we may welcome summer
  As we belong to do."

The Obby Oss is a primitive figure carried by a dancer round the port of Padstow, on the north coast of Cornwall, every year on 1 May to herald the arrival of summer. It is accompanied by music, dancing, and a great deal of merry-making. All the other festivals mentioned are still held in Cornwall: for instance, a chain of bonfires is lit throughout the county on Midsummer Eve, the Eve of St John, since Midsummer Day is also the feast of St John the Baptist.

When the Cornish say that they "belong to" do something, they mean that it is right and proper that something should be done: that it is a personal responsibility.

When I Went Up To Avignon

When I went up to Avignon
With Jean le Bon the butcher's son,
In from the country, and as green,
We signed for seven at seventeen.
Dressed in red and dressed in blue
We walked and talked as the soldiers do.
    Tan-tan-tan!
    Fol-di-ro!

They gave us the gun, they gave us the blade,
They told us the tricks of the soldier's trade.
In rain and snow, in hail and sun,
Our paths were two that had been one,
And many a blow we gave, we bore,
For heavy is the hand of war.
    Tan-tan-tan!
    Fol-di-ro!

When seven long years were lost and won
We came again to Avignon
And I said to Jean of the butcher's knife,
"What shall you do for the rest of life?"
And Jean he smiled and I heard him say,
"My butcher's gear I'll throw away!"
    Tan-tan-tan!
    Fol-di-ro!

"My sharpening steel I'll put in store
And I'll ply the butcher's skill no more.
I'll lay on the fire my butcher's clothes.
I'll grow me a peach, I'll grow me a rose.
I'll grow me the grape till the day I die.
Never ask the reason why."
    Tan-tan-tan!
    Fol-di-ro!

On the Eve of St Thomas

On the Eve of St Thomas
I walked the grey wood
Though mammy she told me
That I never should,

And there did I meet
(Though never one spoke)
Kit-with-the-Canstick,*
The Man in the Oak,

Tom Tumbler and Boneless
And Whistle-the-Fife,
Derrick and Puddlefoot,
Gooseberry Wife,

Changeling, Hob Goblin,
Bull-Beggar and Hag,
Tom Thumb and Puckle,
Long-Jack-with-the-Bag.

They nidded and nodded
And winked me an eye,
They bent and they bowed to me
As I passed by.

Was never a shudder
Nor ever a scream,
The wood was as silent
As it were a dream.

Though still were their voices
Their lips told me clear
They wished me Good Christmas
And many a year.

They never did blatter
Nor shiver nor shriek,
Nor clamour nor yammer
Nor rustle nor screak

As they pointed my path
By bramble and brake,
Waved each a pale hand
As my leave I did take.

And I thought I could tell
As I said them goodbye
Though their lips they did smile
That sad was each eye

As out the grey wood
I went on my way
To hearth and to home
And St Thomas's Day.

In ancient times it was believed that goblins and ghosts of all kinds were likely to be seen particularly between St Thomas's Eve (20 December) and Christmas Eve.

** canstick = candlestick*

Days Before Yesterday

Sexton, Ring the Curfew

Sexton, ring the curfew,
Make the tower sway,
Tell all the children
To come from play.

Ring the bell, sexton,
That everyone may know
It's time for the children
To homeward go.

Here comes Betty,
Here comes May,
Here comes Hetty
Been missing all day.

Here comes Lily,
Here comes Lee,
Here comes Billy
With a cut on his knee.

Here comes Abel,
Here comes Hope,
Here comes Mabel
With a skipping rope.

Here comes Zacky,
Here comes Luke,
Here comes Jackie
With his nose in a book.

Here comes Polly,
Here comes Ruth,
Here comes Molly
With an aching tooth.

Here comes Evie,
Here comes Flo,
Here comes Stevie
With a twisted toe.

Here comes Theo,
Here comes Franz,
Here comes Leo
With a hole in his pants.

Here comes Zoe,
Here comes Jane,
And here's little Joey,
Last again.

When I was a child in my home-town of Launceston the curfew bell (a memory of Norman times) was still rung in the parish church tower for five minutes just after 8 p.m.

Little Lizzie Ivory

Little Lizzie Ivory
Who lives at Uffcombe View
Plays on the grand piano
At the early age of two.

She climbs upon the music stool
With zing and also zest
And spreads out all her pieces
Along the music rest.

She flexes every finger
And then she bends a wrist
In the most distinctive manner
Of the concert pianist.

Her hands fly up, her hands fly down
Just like a music star
In items of all kinds from her
Extensive repertoire.

She plays a guide to Italy,
She plays a guide to Spain
And a table giving times of every
Inter-City train.

She plays the morning paper,
The evening one as well
And a list of wines and spirits
From the landlord of *The Bell*.

She plays a sheet of foolscap
That is absolutely blank
And a paper full of figures
From the Trustee Savings Bank.

She plays the Christmas Catalogue
From Tamplin's Toy Bazaar
And volume one of quite a large
Encyclopaedia.

She plays the birthday letter
She had from Uncle Ned
And the telephone directory
From A right through to Z.

So if Miss Lizzie Ivory
Decides that she must call
To see the shining Steinway
That's just inside the Hall,

Be sure that you have handy
On that very special day
The special sort of music
Miss Lizzie likes to play.

Rise up, Jenny

Rise up, Jenny.
Tidy your bed.
Bring the torn doll
Lies at your head.
  Not today, said Jenny.

Rise up, Jenny.
Go, milk the cow.
Feed the squabble of hens
And the black sow.
  Not today, said Jenny.

Rise up, Jenny.
Hear the school bell.
Time to read, time to count,
Time to spell.
  Not today, said Jenny.

Rise up, Jenny.
Time to cook, time to bake,
Time to wash crocks.
Time to mend, to make.
   Not today, said Jenny.

Rise up, Jenny.
Young man at the gate
Says it's you he will see
Though a year he must wait.
   Not today, said Jenny.

Rise up, Jenny.
Hear the ringing tower.
Take your veil, your white gown
And the orange flower.
   Not today, said Jenny.

Tabitha Tupper

Tabitha Tupper
Had frogs for supper,
Joshua Jones had snails.
Fidelity Flutter
Had seaweed butter
(I think it comes from Wales.)

Jeremy Croop
Had sting-nettle soup
Flavoured with gingerbread.
Dorothy Dart
Had fungus tart
With a kind of chocolate spread.

Timothy Lamb
Had jellyfish jam
Spread with Devonshire cream.
Christopher Hawke
Had bubble-and-squawk
(He said it tasted a dream.)

Nathan Newell
Had winter gruel
That's made from curry and cheese.
William Wade
Had marmalade
Sprinkled with prunes and peas.

But sad to tell
They felt far from well
When they went up to bed,
And "Why it's so
We just don't know!"
Their parents sighed and said,

While Tabitha Tupper
And all the others
Scarcely closed an eye,
And felt ever-so-slightly
Better-go-lightly,
And simply couldn't say why.

Venton Ham

Said Jack to Jim
And Jim to Sam,
"Remember how
The water swam
Over the weir
At Venton Ham?
There we walked,
There we ran,
There we fished
Above the dam.
There we wandered
Up and down
Under the grey eye
Of the town."

Said Jim to Sam
And Sam to Jack,
"In all these years
I've not been back."
"Nor I," said Jack,
"And I declare
We ought to see
How things are there,
For days and months
They hurry on
And come next week
We might be gone."

So Jim and Jack
And also Sam
Hobbled the path
To Venton Ham:
Two with whiskers,
One with a peg
And each as bald
As an ostrich egg.
And all the way
Each mother's son
Nattered and chattered
Of days long done;
Walked and talked
The hour away
Till there was nothing
More to say.

And Jack and Sam
And also Jim
They sat them by
The river rim.
They sat them where
The water sped
And neither spoke
Nor either said,
And all the day
They sat them there
They thought of times
That vanished were:
And first of spring,
Of autumn come,
Blackthorn winter,
Summer sun.

There was no need
To say a word
As each perched easy
As a bird
And watched where
The sweet water sang
Over the weir
At Venton Ham;
Over the weir
Falling free
Down the long valley
To the sea.

Jeremy Peep

Jeremy Peep
When fast asleep
Walks the level
And walks the steep
Eyes tight shut
And face quite pale
His night-shirt billowing
Like a sail.
Down the stairway
And up the street
With nothing at all
Upon his feet.
His arms out straight
In front of his face
He zigs and zags
All over the place.
He never stumbles,
He never slips,
It's as if he could see
With his finger-tips.
"Don't make him open
As much as an eye,"
The neighbours ever so
Softly sigh,
"Or out of his noddle
His wits will fly!
Just turn him about
And watch him head
Straight back home
To his truckle-bed
And sure and slow
He'll get back in
And draw the covers
Up to his chin."

And the neighbours they tut
About this and that
And say, "Jeremy, Jeremy,
What were you at
When the moon was up
And the stars were few
And the Town Hall clock
Was striking two?
Have you *any* idea
Where you were last night
When most good people
Were tucked up tight?"
"Such questions you ask!"
Says Jeremy Peep.
"So silly they strike me
All of a heap!
Walking the town
So wild and wan
With nothing at all
But my night-shirt on?
I can't understand
Why you think I should keep
Such curious habits,"
Says Jeremy Peep.
"Where was I all last night?

Asleep."

Index of first lines